A BEGINNER'S GUIDE
TO THE
TRADITIONAL
LATIN MASS

A BEGINNER'S GUIDE
TO THE
T R A D I T I O N A L
Latin Mass

DERYA LITTLE

Illustrations by Chris Lewis

Angelico Press

For information, address:
Angelico Press, Ltd.
169 Monitor St.
Brooklyn, NY 11222
www.angelicopress.com

978-1-62138-492-2 pb
978-1-62138-493-9 hb
978-1-62138-494-6 ebook

Cover and book design by
Michael Schrauzer

CONTENTS

WELCOME TO THE
𝕷atin 𝕸ass

BEFORE THE MASS

- First-timers, do not expect to follow along. Actually, it is better to put everything down and simply observe. The rubrics and the structure will become familiar soon. We hope that this guide will help you recognize what is happening without much confusion. Meanwhile, enjoy the sights, the smells and the bells!

- If you have little children, do not hesitate to bring them. You will not be the only parent carrying out a kicking and screaming toddler. Hopefully, some one will greet you with a smile, but don't lose heart if people are evasive and cold. It happens. Not everyone is a morning person.

- Next time you can be the smiling face for someone new, and the cranky guy can go unnoticed.

- Until you feel comfortable, sit behind people who know what they are doing.

- Most parishes will provide booklet missals upon arriving. When the time comes you will be ready to purchase a 1962 Missal; that's when you're ready to sit at the big kids' table.

Prayer of
St. Thomas Aquinas
BEFORE MASS

ALL-POWERFUL AND EVERLASTING GOD, BEHOLD, I approach the sacrament of Thine only-begotten Son, our Lord Jesus Christ. As one infirm, I approach the medicine of life; as one unclean, the fountain of mercy; as one blind, the light of eternal splendor; as one poor and needy, the Lord of heaven and earth. Therefore, I ask Thee, from the abundance of Thine immense generosity, to cure my illness, wash away my uncleanness, illuminate my blindness, enrich my poverty, and clothe my nakedness, that I may receive the Bread of Angels, the King of Kings and Lord of Lords, with such reverence and humility, such contrition and devotion, such purity and faith, such purpose and intention, as may be profitable for the salvation of my soul. Grant, I beg Thee, that I may receive not only the sacrament of the Lord's Body and Blood, but also the reality and power of this sacrament. O most gentle God, grant me so to receive the Body of Thine only-begotten Son, our Lord Jesus Christ, which He took of the Virgin Mary, that I might be worthy to be incorporated into His Mystical Body and counted among His members. O most loving Father, give to me Thy beloved Son, whom I intend to receive now in veiled form on my pilgrimage, that I may one day contemplate Him with unveiled face for all eternity, who with Thee liveth and reigneth in the unity of the Holy Spirit, world without end, *Amen.*

Prayer of
St. Thomas Aquinas
AFTER MASS

I GIVE THANKS TO THEE, O LORD, HOLY FATHER, almighty and eternal God, that Thou hast deigned to feed me, not for any merit of my own, but only out of the kindness of Thy mercy, with the precious Body and Blood of Thy Son, our Lord Jesus Christ. And I humbly pray, let not this holy communion be for me an increase of guilt unto my punishment, but an availing plea unto pardon and salvation. May it be for me an armor of faith and a shield of good will. May it be the emptying out of my vices and the destruction of concupiscence and carnal passion. May it be the increase in me of charity and patience, humility and obedience, and every virtue. May it be a firm defense against the snares of all my enemies, visible and invisible, and the complete calming of my impulses, bodily and spiritual. May it be a firm adherence to Thee, the one true God, and the joyful completion of my life's course. And I beseech Thee: deign to lead me, a sinner, to that ineffable banquet, where Thou, with Thy Son and the Holy Spirit, art the true Light of Thy saints, fullness of satisfied desire, eternal gladness, consummate delight, and perfect happiness. Through the same Christ our Lord, *Amen.*

HOW TO USE THIS GUIDE

T HE PRIEST'S POSITION IN RELATION TO THE altar will tell you what is happening. The illustrations in this guide will show only the priest. Pay attention to him, and you will soon be familiar with the flow.

For **High Mass**, odd-numbered pages explain the flow of the Mass. People's postures are marked in capital letters in the left column, while the priest's movements and prayers are summarized in the right column. (Strictly speaking, there are no laws concerning the peoples' postures in the Old Rite.)

Even-numbered pages provide more detail about the specific part of the Mass.

Low Mass is illustrated at the end.

THE SANCTUARY EXPLAINED

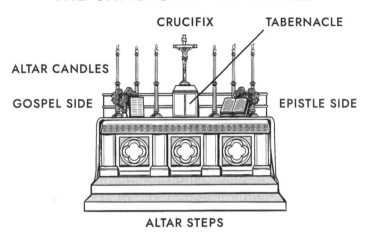

CRUCIFIX   TABERNACLE

ALTAR CANDLES

GOSPEL SIDE   EPISTLE SIDE

ALTAR STEPS

SUNG MASS
(Missa Cantata)

- At least 4 candles lit on the altar
- Priest sings or intones
- Various parts of the Mass are chanted
- The Kyrie, Gloria, Creed, Sanctus and Agnus Dei are sung

LOW MASS
(Quiet Mass)

- 2 candles lit on the altar
- Priest does not sing
- No part of the Mass is chanted
- Hymns may be sung

Solemn Mass, *or* **Solemn High Mass**, *is a type of sung Mass that is celebrated by a priest with a deacon and a subdeacon.*

Ciborium
The ciborium holds the consecrated Hosts.

Chalice
The chalice holds the Precious Blood.

Paten
The priest uses the paten to hold the Host.

High Mass

HIGH MASS

STAND | When the priest enters.

He kneels and prays before the altar.

Asperges Me
*(Sprinkling of Holy Water,
at the principal Mass on Sunday)*

The priest walks down the aisle, blessing everyone.

✝ Bless yourself when you are sprinkled.

KEEP STANDING | Priest returns to the sanctuary to change his vestments.

Now the Mass begins.

THE MASS OF THE CATECHUMENS

THE FIRST PART OF THE MASS, ALSO CALLED THE Mass of the Catechumens, includes the prayers at the foot of the altar, the Introit, the Kyrie, the Gloria, the Collect, the Epistle, the Gradual, the Alleluia or Tract, the Gospel, and the Creed.

People who desire to be baptized are called catechumens (*those who are instructed*). The catechumens used to be dismissed before the Offertory.

Judica Me
(Psalm 42)

Judge me, O God, and distinguish my cause from the nation that is not holy: deliver me from the unjust and deceitful man…

For thou art God my strength…

Send forth thy light and thy truth…

And I will go in to the altar of God: to God who giveth joy to my youth.

To express his desire to approach the altar of the Lord, David wrote this psalm when he was persecuted by Saul. The priest echoes David's words so that he, too, can be free from the attacks of the enemy, sin, and temptation before he ascends to the altar to offer the most Holy Sacrifice.

KNEEL

*You will
be kneeling
for a while.*

In nomine Patris, et Filii, et Spiritus Sancti.
*(In the name of the Father, and of the Son,
and of the Holy Ghost.)*

Judica Me
(Psalm 42)

The priest stands near, but not at the altar.

The Confiteor

(I Confess)

P. I confess to Almighty God, to blessed Mary ever Virgin, to blessed Michael the Archangel, to blessed John the Baptist, to the holy Apostles Peter and Paul, to all the saints, and to you, brethren, that I have sinned exceedingly in thought, word, and deed: (*he strikes his breast three times saying*) through my fault, through my fault, through my most grievous fault. Therefore I beseech blessed Mary ever Virgin, blessed Michael the Archangel, blessed John the Baptist, the holy Apostles Peter and Paul, all the saints, and you, brethren, to pray for me to the Lord our God.

S. I confess to Almighty God, to blessed Mary ever Virgin, to blessed Michael the Archangel, to blessed John the Baptist, to the holy Apostles Peter and Paul, to all the saints, and to you, Father, that I have sinned exceedingly in thought, word, and deed: through my fault, through my fault, through my most grievous fault. Therefore I beseech blessed Mary ever Virgin, blessed Michael the Archangel, blessed John the Baptist, the holy Apostles Peter and Paul, all the saints, and you, Father, to pray for me to the Lord our God.

The priest and the server recite the Confiteor to humbly acknowledge the sin in our lives and thus our need for the Holy Sacrifice. Confession of sins has been a common practice under both the Old and the New Testament prior to offering sacrifices.

YOU ARE
STILL
KNEELING

The Confiteor

- When the priest bows, he is praying the Confiteor.

- When he stands up, he is done and the servers bow and pray the Confiteor as well.

- The priest will briefly bow, say a prayer and then begin to approach the altar.

The Introit
(The Entrance)

THE INTROIT IS THE FIRST PRAYER THE PRIEST reads from the Missal.

This prayer changes according to the feast of the day.

This prayer is the official beginning of the Mass.

The Kyrie

Kyrie Eleison *(Lord, have mercy)*
The first Kyrie is an appeal to the God the Father.

Christe Eleison *(Christ, have mercy)*
This is an appeal to the Anointed Son of God.

Kyrie Eleison *(Lord, have mercy)*
The second Kyrie is an appeal to the Holy Ghost.

"The Father and the Holy Ghost have only the divine nature. But in the Son there is a double nature, the divine and human. To call attention to the Son's human nature we address Him as *Christe*, that is, 'Anointed.' In the second Person of the Blessed Trinity the human nature was anointed, united, with the divine." (Lib. II., *de Myster. Miss.*, cap. 19)

This is the only part of the Mass that is recited in Greek.

**KEEP
KNEELING**

The Introit and the Kyrie

The priest will kiss and incense the altar.

After the incense, he will read the Introit.

Kyrie Eleison will be sung while the priest is praying the Introit.

The Gloria

(The Angelic Hymn)

AFTER THE SUPPLICATION OF THE KYRIE COMES the exultation of the Gloria, which begins with the words of the angelic choir sung at the birth of Our Lord:

> And suddenly there was with the angel a multitude of the heavenly army, praising God, and saying: "Glory to God in the highest; and on earth peace to men of good will." *Luke* 2:13-14

The **Gloria** is also called the **Great Doxology.**

The Gloria is omitted in Masses of the dead and the penitential seasons of Advent and Lent.

The two most common phrases of the Latin Mass are:

> *P.* Dominus vobiscum (*The Lord be with you*).
> *S.* Et cum spiritu tuo (*And with your spirit*).

"The Lord be with you."   *Ruth* 2:4

"The grace of our Lord Jesus Christ be with you." 1 *Cor.* 16:23

"Behold I am with you all days, even to the consummation of the world."   *Matthew* 28:20

"The grace of our Lord Jesus Christ be with your spirit."   *Phil.* 4:23

STAND | ## The Gloria

The priest says the Gloria while it is being sung by the choir.

SIT | The priest finishes the Gloria and takes a seat.

The choir continues singing.

STAND | The priest stands again and returns to the altar when the Gloria is near completion.

The priest turns to the people:

STILL STANDING | *P.* Dominus vobiscum
(*The Lord be with you*).
S. Et cum spiritu tuo
(*And with your spirit*).

The Collect

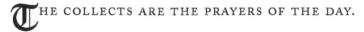

THE COLLECTS ARE THE PRAYERS OF THE DAY.

The priest begins with "Oremus (*Let us pray*)" to invite the faithful to pray with him.

Then he extends his arms in imitation of Moses who prayed on the mountain while the Israelites fought.

The collect ends with the server's "Amen," which is the Hebrew word for "May it be so."

The Epistle

"Epistle" means "letter," because the readings usually are taken from St. Paul's letters.

Both prayer and pious readings prepare us for the Holy Sacrifice.

The Gradual

The Epistle is followed by a Psalm, which used to be chanted on the steps (*gradus*, hence the *Gradual*). Then there is an Alleluia or, in penitential seasons, a Tract.

After the Gradual, the Missal is carried to the left side of the altar, signifying the bringing of the Gospel to the gentiles, and Our Lord's being handed over from one judge to another.

The Collect

The priest moves to the right
side to begin the Collect.

SIT
At Amen

- It will be sung and concluded with
  "Amen."
- People remain seated during the
  Epistle.
- The Gradual and Alleluia (or
  Gradual and Tract) are spoken by
  the priest and chanted by the choir.

The priest moves to the middle
and prepares to sing the Gospel.

The Missal is moved to the
left side for the Gospel.

The Gospel

The Munda Cor Meum
(Cleanse My Heart)

RIGHT BEFORE READING THE GOSPEL, THE PRIEST prays: "Cleanse my heart and my lips, O Almighty God, Who cleansed the lips of the Prophet Isaiah with a burning coal. In Your gracious mercy deign so to purify me that I may worthily proclaim Your holy Gospel."

The people stand for the Gospel out of respect and also to demonstrate their willingness to defend the teachings of Christ.

After the priest announces where the Gospel reading is coming from, he makes the Sign of the Cross on his forehead, lips, and heart, asking the Lord that we may know His Gospel with our minds, profess it with our lips, and follow it with our hearts.

As a sign of reverence, the priest kisses the Gospel once he is done reading.

Even though it is not part of the Mass, the priest gives a homily explaining the Gospel of the day on Sundays and holy days of obligation.

STAND

when the priest sings "Dominus vobiscum."

The Gospel

The priest sings "Dominus vobiscum."

The Gospel is chanted.

Homily

The priest moves the Missal to the middle.

SIT

when the priest reaches the pulpit

He takes off at least his maniple and moves to the pulpit for the homily.

The Epistle and the Gospel are often read in the vernacular.

The Creed

THE CREED IS THE SUMMARY OF THE CHRISTIAN faith and the response of the faithful to the Gospel:

> Credo in unum Deum, Patrem omnipotentem, factorem coeli et terrae, visibilium omnium et invisibilium. Et in unum Dominum Jesum Christum, Filium Dei unigenitum. Et ex Patre natum ante omnia saecula. Deum de Deo, lumen de lumine, Deum verum de Deo vero. Genitum, non factum, consubstantialem Patri: per quem omnia facta sunt. Qui propter nos homines, et propter nostram salutem descendit de coelis. Et incarnatus est de Spiritu Sancto ex Maria Virgine: ET HOMO FACTUS EST. Crucifixus etiam pro nobis sub Pontio Pilato, passus, et sepultus est. Et resurrexit tertia die, secundum Scripturas. Et ascendit in coelum: sedet ad dexteram Patris. Et iterum venturus est cum gloria judicare vivos et mortuos: cujus regni non erit finis. Et in Spiritum Sanctum, Dominum et vivificantem: qui ex Patre Filioque procedit. Qui cum Patre et Filio simul adoratur et conglorificatur: qui locutus est per Prophetas. Et unam, sanctam, catholicam et apostolicam Ecclesiam. Confiteor unum baptisma in remissionem peccatorum. Et exspecto resurrectionem mortuorum. Et vitam venturi saeculi. *Amen.*

If the priest finishes reading the Creed at the altar before the choir finishes he goes to his seat, and when he sits, so do the people.

STILL
SITTING

The Creed

The priest leaves the pulpit and puts the vestments back on.

He approaches the altar for the Creed.

STAND

The Creed begins.

KNEEL
at this part
of the Creed

Et incarnatus est de Spiritu Sancto ex Maria Virgine: ET HOMO FACTUS EST.

STAND

Continue with the rest of the Creed.

The priest may return to his chair during the Creed.

Then, he returns to the altar.

P. Dominus vobiscum.
S. Et cum spiritu tuo.

SIT
After Oremus

P. Oremus.

He recites the Offertory antiphon; the choir sings it.

THE MASS OF THE FAITHFUL

The Offertory

IN THE ANCIENT CHURCH, ALONG WITH BREAD and wine, people brought fruits, oil, wax, and money in support of the clergy.

The priest asks the Lord to accept our offerings despite our unworthiness:

> Accept, O Holy Father, Almighty and eternal God, this spotless host, which I, your unworthy servant, offer to You, my living and true God, to atone for my numberless sins, offenses, and negligences; on behalf of all here present and likewise for all faithful Christians living and dead, that it may profit me and them as a means of salvation to life everlasting.

The Lavabo
(I Will Wash)

After offering the bread and wine, the priest washes his hands before the consecration.

> I will wash my hands among the innocent; and will compass thy altar, O Lord:

> That I may hear the voice of thy praise: and tell of all thy wondrous works.   *Psalm* 25:6-7

**STILL
SITTING**

THE MASS OF THE FAITHFUL
The Offertory

The priest offers the host in the middle of the altar.

He moves to the right to mix the wine with water.

He returns to the middle and continues to pray.

Next, the priest incenses the bread and the wine, followed by the crucifix and the altar.

STAND
*momentarily
for the incense*

The server incenses the people.

SIT

The Lavabo
(The Washing of Hands)

On the right side of the altar, the priest washes his hands and prays before returning to the middle.

Prayer to the Holy Trinity

THE PRIEST QUIETLY PRAYS:

Accept, most Holy Trinity, this offering which we are making to You in remembrance of the passion, resurrection, and ascension of Jesus Christ, Our Lord; and in honor of Blessed Mary, ever Virgin, Blessed John the Baptist, the Holy Apostles Peter and Paul, and of these (*the saints whose relics are in the altar*) and of all the Saints; that it may add to their honor and aid our salvation; and may they deign to intercede in heaven for us who honor their memory here on earth. Through the same Christ our Lord.

The Orate Fratres

This is the last time the priest turns to the people until Communion.

He is like the high priest who leaves to enter the Holy of Holies.

The priest is unworthy of offering this sacrifice, thus is in need of prayers.

The Secret

These prayers are said quietly by the priest.

STILL
SITTING

Prayer to the Holy Trinity

The priest is still at the middle of the altar.

You may not see what he is doing or hear what he is saying.

The Orate Fratres

The priest says "Orate fratres" (*Pray brethren*).

The Secret

This prayer wil be inaudible and will conclude the offertory.

The Preface

THE PRIEST, IN THE PERSON OF CHRIST, ASKS US to dismiss all worldly thoughts in preparation for the Holy Sacrifice:

> *P.* Dominus vobiscum (*The Lord be with you*)
> *S.* Et cum spiritu tuo (*And with your spirit*)
>
> *P.* Sursum corda (*Hearts aloft!*)
> *S.* Habemus ad Dominum (*We have, to the Lord!*)
>
> *P.* Gratias agamus Domino Deo nostro (*Let us give thanks to the Lord our God*)
> *S.* Dignum et justum est (*It is right and just*)

The preface introduces the Canon of the Mass (*the fixed prayer from the Sanctus to the Pater Noster*).

The Sanctus is the canticle of angels seen by the Prophet Isaiah:

> Upon it stood the seraphims: the one had six wings, and the other had six wings: with two they covered his face, and with two they covered his feet, and with two they flew.
>
> And they cried one to another, and said: Holy, holy, holy, the Lord God of hosts, all the earth is full of his glory.   *Isaiah* 6:2-3

The rest comes from Christ's triumphal entry to Jerusalem on Palm Sunday:

> And the multitudes that went before and that followed, cried, saying: Hosanna to the son of David: Blessed is he that cometh in the name of the Lord: Hosanna in the highest.   *Matthew* 21:9

The Canon

STAND The priest, while still facing the altar with his hands outstretched, will chant:

P. Dominus vobiscum
S. Et cum spiritu tuo

P. Sursum corda
S. Habemus ad Dominum

P. Gratias agamus Domino Deo nostro
S. Dignum et justum est

 The **Sanctus** will be sung by the choir.

KNEEL
When the bells ring

While the choir sings, the priest will bow low over the altar and silently pray.

After the choir stops, the priest continues to pray.

 Bells ring, indicating that the consecration will soon follow.

The Canon of the Mass

ONCE THE SANCTUS IS SUNG, THE PRIEST PRAYS the first prayer of the canon, **Te Igitur**, where he makes the Sign of the Cross over the oblation three times.

The **Memento of the Living** is the second prayer of the canon, where we pray for the living.

During the **Communicantes**, the priest asks for the intercession of the Church Triumphant.

During the next two prayers, the priest quietly begs the Lord to accept the offerings and makes the Sign of the Cross five times over the gifts.

At consecration, the priest obeys Christ's command during the Last Supper.

He, *in persona Christi*, can only perform his duty through the Sacrament of Holy Orders.

When the priest takes the Host *(from the Latin word "hostia" meaning "victim")* in his hands for the first time, he will whisper the words of consecration "HOC EST ENIM CORPUS MEUM." This is the solemn moment of Sacrifice.

Transubstantiation takes place at consecration. The priest elevates the Host above his head for the adoration and worship of the faithful.

**KEEP
KNEELING**

HOC EST ENIM CORPUS MEUM
(This is My Body).

Bells will ring after the priest pronounces the words of consecration and genuflects.

Bells will ring at the elevation of the Sacred Host.

Bells will ring when the priest genuflects again to Our Lord.

S IMILARLY, THE PRIEST WHISPERS THE WORDS of consecration over the Chalice and elevates the Blood of Christ for the adoration of the faithful.

There are no longer the substances of bread and wine on the altar. Through the miracle and promise of Christ, the bread has become the Body and wine has become the Blood of Our Lord. By concomitance, the whole Christ, risen and glorified, is present under the species (appearances) of both the bread and the wine.

During consecration, the priest acts as Christ Himself, which is why he leans into the altar in an intimate manner.

> The same night in which he was betrayed, he took bread. And giving thanks, broke, and said: Take ye, and eat: this is my body, which shall be delivered for you: this do for the commemoration of me.

> In like manner also the chalice, after he had supped, saying: This chalice is the new testament in my blood: this do ye, as often as you shall drink, for the commemoration of me.

> For as often as you shall eat this bread, and drink the chalice, you shall show the death of the Lord, until he come.   1 *Cor.* 11:23-26

KEEP KNEELING

HIC EST ENIM CALIX SANGUINIS MEI *(For this is the chalice of My Blood).*

Bells will ring after the priest pronounces the words of consecration and genuflects.

Bells will ring at the elevation of the Precious Blood.

Bells will ring when the priest genuflects again to Our Lord.

Communion

The Our Father

Pater noster, qui es in coelis: sanctificetur nomen tuum: adveniat regnum tuum: fiat voluntas tua, sicut in coelo et in terra. Panem nostrum quotidianum da nobis hodie: et dimitte nobis debita nostra, sicut et nos dimittimus debitoribus nostris. Et ne nos inducas in tentationem: sed libera nos a malo. *Amen.*

The Host broken over the Chalice symbolizes the death of Our Lord and His Precious Blood flowing from His broken body. In order to eliminate any illusion that the Lord's Body and Blood are separated, the priest drops a piece of the Host in the Precious Blood. Our Lord is fully present under both species.

Ecce, Agnus Dei

The next day, John saw Jesus coming to him, and he saith: Behold the Lamb of God, behold him who taketh away the sin of the world.   *John* 1:29

Domine, non sum dignus

Lord, I am not worthy that Thou shouldst enter under my roof; but only say the word, and my soul shall be healed. *(Repeated three times.)*   *Matthew* 8:8

KEEP KNEELING

The priest continues to pray, including praying for the dead and for fellowship with the saints.

The priest genuflects.

STAND
When the priest says "Oremus"

Communion

The priest prays the Pater Noster *(Our Father)*.

"Sed libera nos a malo" is chanted by all.

KNEEL

The priest mixes a particle of the Host with the Precious Blood.

The priest will consume Our Lord's Body and Blood.

He will turn with the Host towards the people and say: "Ecce Agnus Dei" *(Behold the Lamb of God)*.

The priest will give communion to those serving at the altar.

The faithful may approach the altar rails to receive Our Lord KNEELING and on the TONGUE.

A server will hold the paten under your chin while the priest places the Host on your tongue. Tilt back your head, open your mouth, and stick out your tongue. No need to say *"Amen."*

Communion Antiphon

EVERY COMMUNICANT WHO WAS IN A STATE OF grace before communion is now sacramentally united with Christ. Spend the next fifteen minutes in thanksgiving, praise, and adoration. The Real Presence of Our Lord will remain within one's body as long as the appearances of the bread remain, which is about fifteen minutes.

The priest purifies the chalice and returns to the Epistle side to read a short Scripture verse called the Communion Antiphon.

> For this is my blood of the new testament, which shall be shed for many unto remission of sins.

> And I say to you, I will not drink from henceforth of this fruit of the vine, until that day when I shall drink it with you new in the kingdom of my Father.

> And a hymn being said, they went out unto Mount Olivet.   *Matthew* 26:28-30

KNEEL

After Communion

Return to your pew and kneel.

After everyone has received, the priest returns to the altar to put the ciborium in the tabernacle.

The priest will cleanse his fingers and the chalice.

STAND

The priest returns to the middle and turns towards the people to say "Dominus vobiscum."

The priest returns to the right side and prays the Postcommunion prayer.

He returns to the middle and turns to the people: "Dominus vobiscum."

The Dismissal

While facing the faithful, he says "Ite, Missa est" *(Go, it is sent)*.

KNEEL

The priest turns to the altar for a prayer.

He gives the Last Blessing.

The Last Gospel

THE LAST GOSPEL USED TO BE A PRIVATE PRAYER said by the priest in the sacristy, but because of the reverence paid to this Scripture passage by Christians, it became part of the Mass:

> In the beginning was the Word, and the Word was with God, and the Word was God. The same was in the beginning with God. All things were made by Him, and without Him was made nothing that was made. In Him was life, and the life was the light of men: and the light shineth in darkness, and the darkness did not comprehend it.

> But as many as received Him, to them He gave great power to become the sons of God: to them that believe in His name: who are born, not of blood, nor of the will of the flesh, nor of the will of man, but of God. And *(here all genuflect)* THE WORD WAS MADE FLESH, AND DWELT AMONG US, and we saw His glory, the glory as of the only begotten of the Father, full of grace and truth.   *John* 1:1-14

STAND

The Last Gospel

After the Last Blessing, the priest kisses the altar, turns to people and says: "Dominus vobiscum."

He blesses the people with the Sign of the Cross.

He reads the Last Gospel on the left side of the altar.

YOU ALSO GENUFLECT

Keep your eyes on the priest, because he will genuflect at "ET VERBUM CARO FACTUM EST."

STAND

The priest returns to the middle, but at the bottom of the altar where the Mass started.

The Mass has ended and the priest exits the sanctuary.

Low Mass

LOW MASS

STAND When the priest enters.

He genuflects and prays before the altar.

KNEEL
Until the Gospel
✠

In nomine Patris, et Filii, et Spiritus Sancti.
*(In the Name of the Father, and of the Son,
and of the Holy Ghost.)*

Judica Me
(Psalm 42)

The priest stands near, but not at the
altar yet.

The Confiteor

- When the priest bows, he is praying the Confiteor.

- When he stands up, he is done and the servers bow and pray the Confiteor as well.

- The priest will briefly bow, say a prayer and then begin to approach the altar.

The Introit and the Kyrie

The priest will kiss the altar.

The priest will read the Introit.

Kyrie Eleison.

The Gloria

The priest says the Gloria.

P. Dominus vobiscum
   (*The Lord be with you*).
S. Et cum spiritu tuo
   (*And with your spirit*).

The Collect

The priest moves to the right side to say the Collect. It will be concluded with "Amen."

The Epistle

The Gradual and the Alleluia or Tract are spoken by the priest.

The Missal is moved to the left side for the Gospel.

STAND

when the priest says "Dominus vobiscum."

The Gospel

The priest says "Dominus vobiscum."

The Gospel reading begins.

Homily

The priest moves the Missal to the middle of the altar.

SIT

when the priest reaches the pulpit

If there is to be preaching, he takes off his maniple and moves to the pulpit for the homily.

The Epistle and the Gospel are often read in the vernacular.

STILL
SITTING

The Creed

The priest leaves the pulpit and returns to the altar, where he puts on the maniple.

If it is a Sunday or a major feast, he recites the Creed.

STAND The Creed begins.

KNEEL
at this part
of the Creed

Et incarnatus est de Spiritu Sancto ex Maria Virgine: ET HOMO FACTUS EST.

STAND Continue with the rest of the Creed.

P. Dominus vobiscum.
S. Et cum spiritu tuo.

SIT
After Oremus

P. Oremus.

The priest recites the Offertory antiphon.

*In some places,
bells are rung.*

The Mass of the Faithful

The Offertory

The priest offers the host in the middle
of the altar.

He moves to the right to mix the wine
with water.

He returns to the middle and continues
to pray.

The Lavabo
(The Washing of Hands)

On the right side of the altar, the priest
washes his hands and prays before
returning to the middle.

STILL
SITTING

Prayer to the Most Holy Trinity

The priest is still at the middle of the altar.

STILL
SITTING

The Orate Fratres

The Secret

Said in silence.

The Canon

KNEEL
When the bells ring

Sanctus will be recited.

Canon: The priest will bow low over the altar and silently pray.

Bells ring, indicating that the consecration will soon follow.

KEEP KNEELING

HOC EST ENIM CORPUS MEUM *(This is My Body)*.

Bells will ring after the priest pronounces the words of consecration and genuflects.

Bells will ring at the elevation of the Sacred Host.

Bells will ring when the priest genuflects again to Our Lord.

KEEP KNEELING

HIC EST ENIM CALIX SANGUINIS MEI *(For this is the chalice of My Blood).*

Bells will ring after the priest pronounces the words of consecration and genuflects.

Bells will ring at the elevation of the Precious Blood.

Bells will ring when the priest genuflects again to Our Lord.

KNEEL

Communion

The priest prays the Pater Noster *(Our Father)*.

The priest mixes a particle of the Host with the Precious Blood.

The priest will consume Our Lord's Body and Blood.

He will turn with the Host towards the people and say: "Ecce Agnus Dei" *(Behold the Lamb of God)*.

The priest will give communion to those serving at the altar.

The faithful may approach the altar rails to receive Our Lord KNEELING and on the TONGUE.

A server will hold the paten under your chin while the priest places the Host on your tongue. Tilt back your head, open your mouth, and stick out your tongue. No need to say "Amen."

KNEEL

After Communion

Return to your pew and kneel.

After everyone has received, the priest returns to the altar to put the ciborium in the tabernacle.

The priest will cleanse his fingers and the chalice.

STAND

The priest returns to the middle and turns towards the people to say "Dominus vobiscum."

The priest returns to the right side and prays the Postcommunion prayer.

He returns to the middle and turns to the people: "Dominus vobiscum."

The Dismissal

While facing the faithful, he says "Ite, Missa est" *(Go, it is sent)*.

KNEEL

The priest turns to the altar for a prayer.

He gives the Last Blessing.

STAND	# The Last Gospel

After the Last Blessing, the priest kisses the altar, turns to people and says: "Dominus vobiscum."

He blesses the people with the Sign of the Cross.

He reads the Last Gospel on the left side of the altar.

YOU ALSO GENUFLECT

Keep your eyes on the priest, because he will genuflect at "ET VERBUM CARO FACTUM EST."

STAND

The priest descends to the bottom of the altar where the Mass started.

KNEEL

Prayers After Low Mass

Depending on your parish, the people kneel and the priest leads the faithful in prayer.

Hail Mary (*prayed 3 times*)
Hail, Holy Queen
Priest: O God, our refuge and our strength…
All: Amen.
Saint Michael prayer
Priest: Most Sacred Heart of Jesus,
All: Have mercy on us. (*prayed 3 times*)

The Mass has ended and the priest exits the sanctuary.

Latin Prayers

Sign of the Cross

IN NOMINE PATRIS, ET Filii, et Spiritus Sancti. *Amen.*

IN THE NAME OF THE Father, and of the Son, and of the Holy Ghost. *Amen.*

The Lord's Prayer

PATER NOSTER, qui es in caelis, sanctificetur nomen tuum. Adveniat regnum tuum. Fiat voluntas tua, sicut in caelo et in terra. Panem nostrum quotidianum da nobis hodie, et dimitte nobis debita nostra sicut et nos dimittimus debitoribus nostris. Et ne nos inducas in tentationem, sed libera nos a malo. *Amen.*

OUR FATHER, who art in heaven, hallowed be thy name; thy kingdom come; thy will be done on earth as it is in heaven. Give us this day our daily bread; and forgive us our trespasses as we forgive those who trespass against us; and lead us not into temptation but deliver us from evil. *Amen.*

The Hail Mary

AVE MARIA, gratia plena, Dominus tecum. Benedicta tu in mulieribus, et benedictus fructus ventris tui, Iesus. Sancta Maria, Mater Dei, ora pro nobis peccatoribus, nunc et in hora mortis nostrae. *Amen.*

HAIL MARY, full of grace; the Lord is with thee; blessed art thou among women, and blessed is the fruit of thy womb, Jesus. Holy Mary, Mother of God, Pray for us sinners, now and at the hour of our death. *Amen.*

Glory Be

GLORIA PATRI, et Filio, et Spiritui Sancto. Sicut erat in principio, et nunc, et semper, et in saecula saeculorum. *Amen.*

GLORY BE TO THE FATHER, and to the Son, and to the Holy Ghost; as it was in the beginning, is now, and will be for ever. *Amen.*

Hail, Holy Queen

SALVE REGINA, Mater misericordiae. Vita, dulcedo, et spes nostra, salve. Ad te clamamus exsules filii Hevae. Ad te suspiramus, gementes et flentes in hac lacrimarum valle. Eia ergo, Advocata nostra, illos tuos misericordes oculos ad nos converte. Et Iesum, benedictum fructum ventris tui, nobis post hoc exsilium ostende. O clemens, o pia, o dulcis Virgo Maria.

V. Ora pro nobis, Sancta Dei Genitrix.

℟. Ut digni efficiamur promissionibus Christi.

HAIL, HOLY QUEEN, Mother of mercy! Hail, our life, our sweetness, and our hope! To you do we cry, poor banished children of Eve. To you do we send up our sighs, mourning, and weeping in this valley of tears. Turn then, most gracious advocate, your eyes of mercy toward us; and after this, our exile, show unto us the blessed fruit of your womb, Jesus. O clement, O loving, O sweet Virgin Mary!

V. Pray for us, O Holy Mother of God.

℟. That we may be made worthy of the promises of Christ.

THE NEXT STEP

To ENTER MORE DEEPLY INTO THE PRAYERS OF the traditional Latin Mass, you will eventually want to obtain a daily Missal that contains all of the prayers, fixed and changing, for every day of the year. When you get your first Missal, it can seem overwhelming. Where do you even begin?

The book is thick and will most likely include four or five colored ribbons. Begin by placing your ribbons outside of the book pages and open to the Table of Contents. You will see that this Missal is more than a guidebook to the Mass. It has devotions, prayers, summaries of Catholic doctrine, and sometimes even Gregorian chants. It is a goldmine of Catholic spirituality. Peruse the table of contents and become familiar with what it contains.

For now, let's keep it simple and use your ribbons. (Prayer cards also make good bookmarks in a Missal.) Here's one way to set them up.

The Liturgical Calendar should be towards the beginning of the Missal. You might place the *first ribbon* here. Some dates may be labelled "feria," which simply means a day of the week on which no feast is assigned. On those days, either the preceding Sunday Mass is prayed again, or a votive Mass may be used.

Your *second ribbon* could be placed in the "Proper of the Season." This part of the book follows the Church year through its major seasons: Advent, Christmas, Epiphany, Septuagesima, Lent, Easter, Ascension, and Pentecost. Here you will find the Sunday "Propers," that is, the antiphons, readings, and prayers used at Mass. (Low and High Mass will share the same propers.)

The 1962 Missal uses a one-year cycle of readings. For example, let's say it's summer and after Pentecost. You discover the upcoming weekend is the Tenth Sunday after Pentecost from your church bulletin. After consulting your Missal's Table of Contents, you'll find where the *Proper of the Season* section begins. Locate *Tenth Sunday After Pentecost.* There you will see Introit, Collect, Epistle, Gradual, Alleluia, Gospel, Offertory, Secret, Communion, Postcommunion. Once the Mass begins, you'll be flipping back to this ribboned section.

The *third ribbon* could be placed at the beginning of the *Order of the Mass*—either at "Preparation for Holy Mass," the "Asperges Me," or the "Mass of the Catechumens." As the Mass proceeds, you can use the ribbon to keep your place in the Mass while you flip to where the Propers are located.

The *fourth ribbon* should be placed in the *Proper of the Saints*. This section will most likely be found after the Order of Mass. Most calendar dates will have a corresponding saint to be celebrated. You will use this section much the same way as the Proper of the Season; it will have the same Mass Propers (Introit through Postcommunion), although sometimes it will give you a page number of a "Common" of a certain category of saint, since relatively few saints have Mass texts unique to themselves.

Other popular sections include "Devotions for Communion," "Feasts of the Blessed Virgin," and "Various Devotions." The biggest hurdle is getting started. Start with the Mass, and the rest will fall into place!

9 781621 384922